I0804767

Allied Aircraft Art

A-10A Thunderbolt II, irreverently nicknamed "Warthog." We see here the business end of the **Thunderbolt II**, complete with shark's teeth and cannon, bombs on pylons and target designed engine dust and f.o.d. covers. This aircraft serial 80-0186 is assigned to the 23rd TFW. *James*

Nose Art, Paint Schemes & Unusual Markings on Aircraft From Korea to Desert Storm

John M. & Donna Campbell

Schiffer Military History
West Chester, PA

Acknowledgements

The completion of another aviation project is always a joy as well as a relief. We must always bear in mind that there are always contributing factors to the success of any photo journal. Good ideas, good photographs and great contributors are essential to a good book, a great publisher and his staff really helps. In listing the names of those to whom we are forever in debt for their help with this project, will begin with of course Bob Biondi for his interest in this project and bringing it to light before its conception. We must thank Nancy & Peter Schiffer, the publishers, for their patience, encouragement, support and quality control, and also their staff. We would like to express our profound gratitude to the donors of countless photographs which enabled us to amass this combination aircraft paint scheme and nose art book that is unusual to the norm. We wish to thank the men and women of the Kansas Aeronautical Society, especially Mr. John Davis for his expertise in the locating of many fine photos, also A. Kevin Grantham for looking into his sources and to his many friends for aiding us. Our Oklahoma Aviation Hobbyist Connection, Mike Conners, owner of The Hobby Shop in Oklahoma City and also Dallas Texas. Our great appreciation must be expressed to Gary James, who has one of the most complete and comprehensive slide collections in the country, for allowing us unlimited access to it. We wish to pay tribute to the late Robert J. Pickett of Wichita Kansas for shooting slides of aircraft from the year 1946 till the late 1970s and his passing. We must give mention to our fellow writer and historian, Nick Veronico, who has had a positive effluence on our work and our intelligence gathering. While on this intelligence gathering tour we were pleased and lucky to make the acquaintance of Robert Mikesh who also opened his collection to us. Many excellent photographers have been covered in this work including Barry Miller, Ted W. Van Geffen, Job C. Conger, Steve Pace, Don Truax, our friend and associate, Steve Link (the Tinker AFB, line photographer and special projects lineman), Charles Stewart, J.E Rotramel and Don Logan. A very special thanks must go to our friend "MAD" Mike Hill for his contributions and continued support to our aviation efforts. Also Col. Alton Whitley, commander of the 37th TFW, for permitting the use of nose art in the weapons bays on his wing's F-117s during Desert Storm as well as his personal contribution in bringing the F-117 up to par in the test phase of this fine aircraft. We wish to also thank our good friend M/Sgt. Mark Bacon at Elmendorf AFB for his assistance in gathering many of the Desert Storm shots. Our thanks to Maj. S.D. Huff for the beautiful F-4 Phantom II shots. And our thanks to Carmine and Eulene Harber for their support. Our thanks as always must go to our loving parents, Jesse & Jewell Easton who have believed in us and our work and Fay D. & Ruth Campbell who have always been an inspiration and pillar to lean on.

The recurrence of nose art on today's aircraft is a tribute to the spirit of fighting men and we are very proud to have been able to do this small portfolio.

Front Cover

Top: **HORNET,** serial 160775, was McDonnell Douglas' prototype for the first F-18A. We see on the nose a stylized hornet as well as a more comical figure on the vertical leaning against the number 1. *Truax*

Center left: T-33A, serial 0-35326, of the 178th Fighter Interceptor Squadron at Fargo, North Dakota shows the decorative tip tanks and the slogan, **Happy Hooligans.** *Hill*

Center right: Olia ANG. This ship carries the name **The Bald Eagles** along with a painting of the unit's mascot. *KAHS*

Below: This line of F-4s, belonging to the 23rd TFW, founded by the original "Flying Tigers", is flying a mission during Team Spirit out of Clark Field. The 23rd can boast of a long and successful history which has taken them from Burma to Baghdad during the last fifty years. These aircraft are on a hunting trip looking for Soviet Bears off the coast of Korea. *Huff Hill*

Rear Cover

This flying dragon, from the days of King Arthur, was appropriately named **Excalibur**. Note that the sword for which this art was named is also included in the artwork. This B-1B, serial 86-6122, belongs to the 319th BW. This photo was taken on 10 June 1990 at Boscombe Down, England. *James*

Page 1:

This art which appears to be out of the Arabian Nights, was on an EP-3E, serial 157320 belonging to the RAF, Fairford. Note the word "Storm" on the shield denoting its service during Desert Storm. *James*

Book Design by Robert Biondi

Library of Congress Catalog Number: 92-64392.

Printed in the United States of America.
ISBN: 0-88740-444-8

Published by Schiffer Publishing, Ltd.
1469 Morstein Road
West Chester, Pennsylvania 19380
Please write for a free catalog.
This book may be purchased from the publisher.
Please include $2.95 postage.
Try your bookstore first.

Contents

Introduction

For years aviation authors have written the histories, diaries and experiences of the aviators and ground crews of the great planes. They wrote of our historic past, as well as our salty present. Some reference has been given to the nose art as an art form and a way for these pilots, crews, and ground personnel to express themselves freely.

The aircraft of the last twenty years is not too different in retrospect. This publication includes an assortment of paintings, paint schemes, Centennial and Bicentennial designs, all with one thing in common, these works of art and spirit are displayed on the outer skins of the aircraft.

We will tour through paint schemes showing shark's teeth, heavy metal magic, and racy ladies. The reader will journey to Europe to a Tiger Meet, which is an international aircraft competition where tiger and jungle cat paint schemes are the rule and not the exception. A-10 Thunderbolts and F-4 Phantom IIs will take the reader on a

The F-4N, #204, serial 151510, belonging to VF-111 is seen at NAS Whidbey Island, 6 August 1977. *KAHS*

roller coaster ride into the artists imagination. The unconquerable spirit of the American fighting man is still alive, as well as a profound sense of humor. We will take a stroll into Operation Desert Storm, and take a first hand look at the Tornados, Victors, and C-130s which were participants. We will, for perhaps the first time, take a close-up look into the weapons bays of the now infamous F-117 Stealth fighter and the hidden humor of weapons bay art. While in the Middle East we will look at the colorful metaphors painted on the weapons to be delivered to Saddam Hussein, and his tyrannical followers, many of which will carry a familiar tune. We will see a few pieces of rare F-105 Thunderchief bomb bay door art and clever names on the intakes and panels of just about any active duty aircraft of the last twenty years. Sit back and enjoy the tour, we're very happy to have you aboard!

A-7

This A-7D was named **City of Bowie.** The large blade Bowie knife can be seen under the name placard. *James*

This fierce shark mouth design was on an A-7D belonging to the 23rd TFW. *KAHS*

Slovobian AF Sluf, an A-7D, serial 71-0297, was piloted by Capt. J. Fitzpatrick, 125th TFS. Pictured at Tinker AFB. *James*

Dreamer was on an A-7, serial 74-751, belonging to the 125th TFS, Oklahoma Air National Guard, Tulsa. The caption under the art says, "A Pepsi break never hurt anybody!" Note the falling coconut over our dreamer's head. This photo was taken at Tinker AFB, Oklahoma, 24 June 1984. *Bacon*

The question over this painting is **"The Price For Freedom?"** The answer found below is **"You Betcha."** This A-7D, serial 70-0981, belonged to the 125th TFS, OK ANG. Pictured at Tinker AFB, February 1984. *James*

The Mean Machine is on an A7-D, serial 73-014, belonging to the 138th TFG, 125th TFS. Pictured at Tinker AFB, 23 January 1983. *James*

Ezekiel's Eagle is on an A-7D, serial 69-6239, belonging to the 125th TFS, OK ANG. *James*

This A-7D, serial 73-011, is another of the aircraft belonging to the OK ANG. The coffee mug pictured in the art titled **Coffee Break!** carries the name Cowboys and the star that goes along with the OSU insignia. This photo was taken at Tinker AFB, 9 December 1984. *James*

Death Dealer was found on an A-7D, Corsair, serial 70-0966, belonging to the 149th TFS, Virginia Air National Guard, Richmond Va. *James*

Honey Pot 2, an A-7D, serial 69-6197, was assigned to the 149th TFS, VA ANG at Richmond. Note the Leprechaun clinging to the pot o' gold. *James*

Dollar 99, an A-7D, serial 69-6199, served with the 149th TFS. The 99 in the name was taken from the last three numbers in the aircraft's serial, 199. *James*

This little Leprechaun is on a Corsair II, serial 71-364, belonging to the VA ANG and is titled, **The Gambler.** Is our little gambler tempting fate by standing on the number 13, or merely suppressing bad luck? *James*

This heavy-metal art is on an A-7D, serial 72-0249, belonging to the 149th TFS. This logo was also used with a popular alcoholic beverage advertisement. *James*

Play Mate, an A-7D, serial 71-0350, was assigned to the VA ANG, 149th TFS, Richmond. This scantily clad young lady depicts the leisure life on the beach, with good company and a bottle of champagne. *James*

Capt Eddle, named for Capt. Eddie Rickenbacker, a famous World War I ace, adorned this A-7D, serial 73-0999, of the Ohio Air National Guard. *James*

The squadron insignia is proudly on display on this A-7D, serial 72-0254, belonging to the 124th TFS of the Iowa ANG. *James*

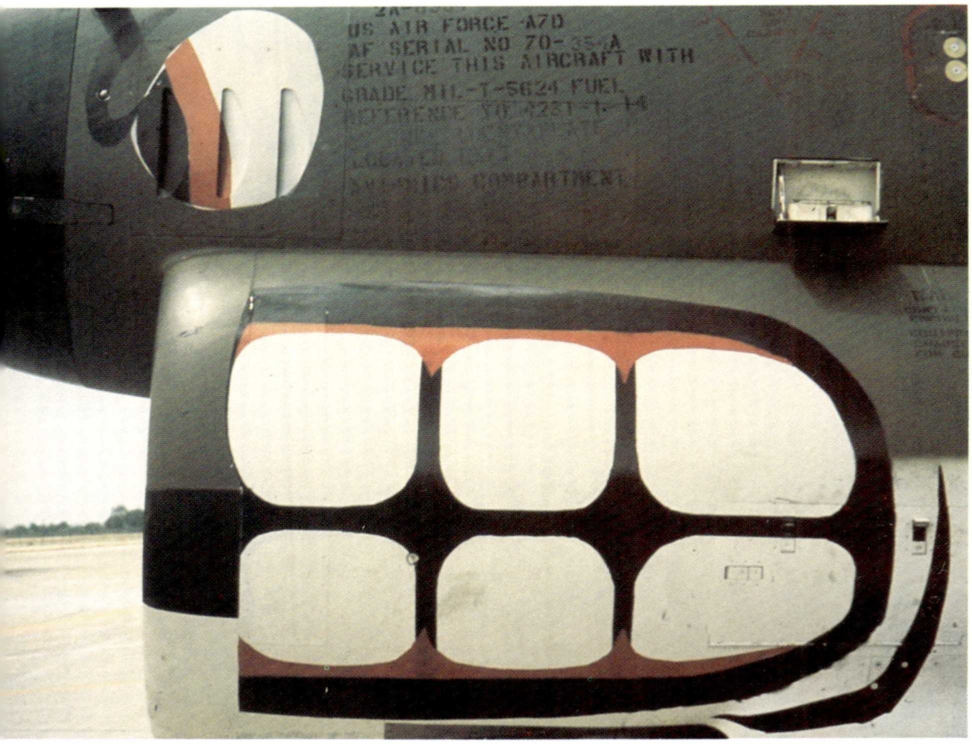

This A-7D, serial 71-354, stationed at Korat, Thailand, seems to be more of a vegetarian due to the grinding molar teeth. This is in sharp contrast to the very popular shark mouths seen often on aircraft. This aircraft was assigned to 354th TFW. *Campbell*

This A-7D, assigned to the 354th TFW at Korat RTAFB, is clearly a meat-eater. This photo was taken January of 1973 as it sat in waiting for the next mission. *Campbell*

The A-7D, **City of Springfield,** serial 72-0178, was assigned to the 162nd TFS of the Ohio ANG and was piloted by Col. R. Higgins. *James*

Thumper, an A-7D, serial 71-0374, belonging to the 149th TFS, VA ANG. This popular WWII art is just as welcome on today's aircraft as it was on the prop-jobs of WWII. Thumper is the cartoon character from Walt Disney's creation "Bambi." *James*

A-7D's are affectionately called SLUF by their contemporaries meaning, Slow Little Ugly #*?! (Fellow?). This A-7D, serial 73-0997, was assigned to the 146th TFS at RAF Fairford. It sports the title, **1991 Stanley Cup Champs,** and a painting of the Pittsburgh Penguins Ice Hockey Club Logo. *James*

Here we see another A-7D of the 146th TFS at RAF Fairford, England. The art depicted on this aircraft, serial 71-0362, is a dedication to the **Pittsburgh Pirates,** 1991 National League Division Champs in baseball. *James*

Rebel Rider, an A-7K, serial 80-0288, belongs to the VA ANG, 149th TFS. The art depicts a Confederate charge during the Civil War with the squadron insignia slightly above. *James.*

This A-7D of the Colorado ANG, serial 70-986, bears witness to their victory at **Gunsmoke 1981,** where they won the world championship at the fighter weapons meet. This aircraft was piloted by Dana Alexander of the 120th TFS. *James*

Yoxford Boys, this A-7D, was named for the members of the 357th Fighter Group which served in England during World War II. This SLUF is assigned to the 162nd TFS, Ohio ANG. *James*

Tailwind, an A-7D, serial 72-0240, of the 149th TFS Virginia ANG, Richmond. The painting depicts a style of art which was common during World War II. *James*

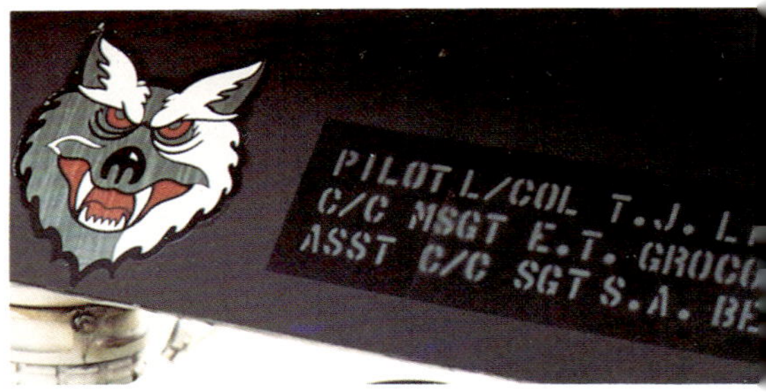

The nose wheel door is an excellent place to paint the wolves head insignia of the South Dakota Air Guard. This A-7D, serial 70-933, was piloted by Lt.Col. T.J. Lien of the 175th TFS. *James*

As seen here, the art from the aircraft often found its way on to other objects. This time it was on this helmet belonging to a member of the 149th TFS, VA ANG. *Watts*

Virginia Gentleman, serial 70-0979, was assigned to the 149th TFS, VA ANG, Richmond. Many aircraft simply have a stylish name adorning them. *James*

This A-7D, serial 73-004, is seen in lizard camouflage. Note the rather ornate external fuel tank in red, white and blue. Our stars and bars seem to illuminate the picture with a patriotic flare. *James*

Little Sweetie 4, an A-7D, serial 71-169, belonged to the 162nd TFS, Ohio ANG. *Hill*

This shark mouth A-7B, serial 154371, belonged to VA 203. Seen here while visiting Dallas Naval Air Station. *KAHS*

A-10

Bavaria, an A-10A, serial 78-685, seen here with a Stuttgart style of lion on its nose. *James*

Tiger 1, with the art on the crew ladder door, depicts the tiger of the 23rd TFW. This A-10A, serial 82-665, seen here in England. *James*

KC "Hawg's", an A-10A of the 303rd TFS, 442nd TFW, serial 78-0605, was photographed at RAF Woodbridge, England. The art pictures an A-10 coming in ready for bear. This is another example of crew ladder hatch art. *James*

Swine Trek, an A-10A, serial 78-0708, served with 103rd TFS Pennsylvania ANG. The art was inspired by the aircraft's nickname. The name was due to the TV program *Star Trek*. The two of these created a humorous combination. The hog has its cannon in its snout and the twin turbofans on its back as does its namesake. *James*

Battlin Badger, an A-10A, serial 77-0184, was assigned to the 45th TFS, Grissom AFB, Indiana. The art is a badger in mechanics coveralls with wrench at-the-ready and is also painted on the crew ladder hatch. *James*

Death from Above! A winged avenger, apparently a bat with female warrior depicted in this medieval scene, hails death and destruction. This A-10A assigned to the 81st TFS serial 80-0147 is pictured at RAF Bentwaters. *James*

Panther, an A-10A, Thunderbolt II, of the 353rd TFS, as it is depicted on the crew ladder hatch, of a/c serial 79-100. *James*

Gunsmoke, the art on the crew ladder hatch depicts the number one fighter weapons meet in the U.S.A. where all of the best-of-the-best, fighter aircraft and ground crews go to compete for that title. This aircraft of the 354th TFW, serial 78-0714, is seen here in immaculate form. *James*

The A-10A, serial 81-0959, sends its message with an internationally recognizable insignia. This one depicting, "no tanks." The A-10A is particularly gifted at tank busting what with the rapid firing armor piercing cannon. *James*

This A-10A, of the 81st TFW, serial 82-0655, was assigned to RAF Woodbridge, England. We see Garfield the cat in the "catbird seat" zooming in on his arch rival, a rather surprised looking canine. This art was painted on the crew ladder hatch. *James*

The A-10A, **Under A Blood Red Sky,** serial 81-0962, was assigned to the 81st TFW at RAF Woodbridge, England. Pictured here we see a demonic figure attacking a Russian tank with its claws firing down on the tank. The A-10A is a purveyor of tank busting. *James*

Hog 6 was the art found on the travel pod under the A-10A, serial 81-946. *James*

Left This A-10A of the 81st TFW, serial 80-0181, based at RAF Bentwaters, bears the futuristic paint scheme of an H.G. Wells inspired war machine. *James*

Sunset Splendor, an A-10A, serial 77-0239, of the 45th TFS, Indiana ANG, at Grissom AFB. This art seems to contradict the purpose of the aircraft it is on. It produces a strong feeling of peace as we see the tropical sunset with the couple together on the beach taking a romantic walk in the twilight. *James*

Party Time at the Bistro, an A-10A of the 81st TFW, serial 81-0978, was based at RAF Woodbridge. This femme fatale painted on the crew ladder hatch is certainly a nice piece of work, perhaps the artist desires the company of a female and a drink. *James*

A View to a Kill, an A-10A, serial 78-680, of the 353rd TFS at Myrtle Beach, S.C. During WWII many females were seen riding various forms of bombs, none as sophisticated as this Maverick missile. *James*

Right The A-10A, serial 78-700, is marked with this fighting crow. *Campbell*

Heat Seeker an A-10A, serial 80-0236, was assigned to the 81st TFW at RAF Woodbridge, England. The name says it all on this more risque art that is reminiscent of the humor or innuendo contained in the art of WWII. *James*

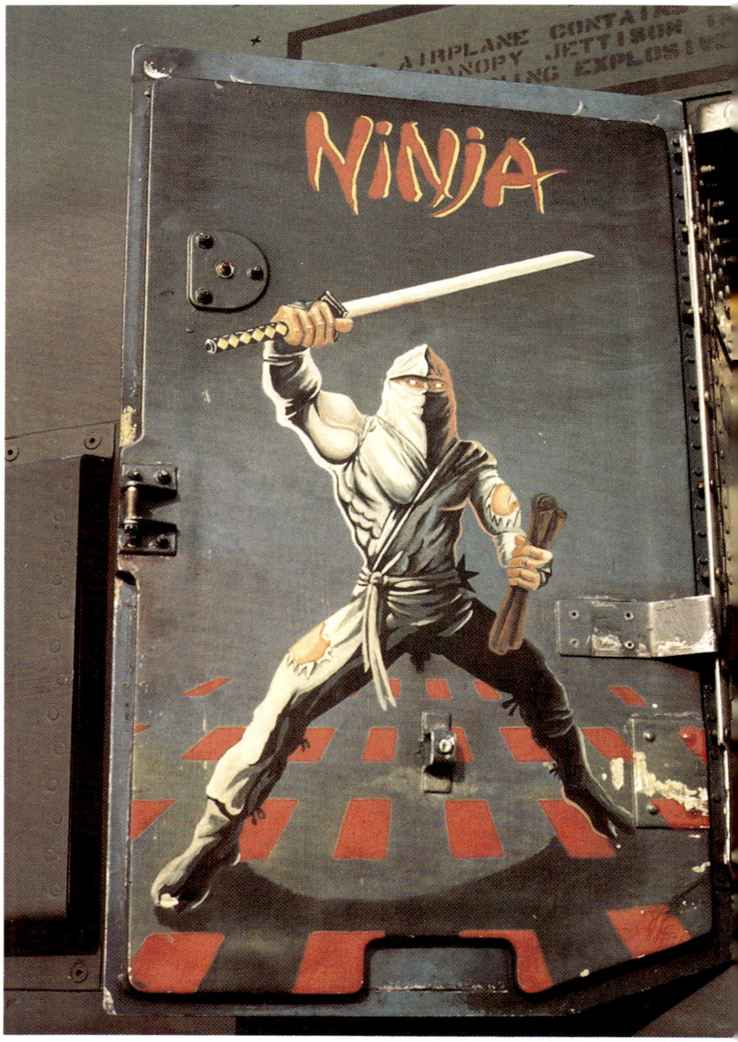

Ninja, an A-10A, serial 80-0204, of the 81st TFW at RAF Woodbridge. This generation of aviation crews has its own heroes-of-the-day. One of which is pictured on the crew ladder hatch of this Thunder Bolt II. *James*

Above: **Fairbanks,** an OA-10, is from the 18th TFS at Eielson AFB, Fairbanks, Alaska. *Bacon*

Left A beautiful American Bald Eagle perched on high adorns the crew ladder hatch on the A-10A, serial 78-0685. *Campbell*

In keeping with the name Warthog, this A-10A, serial 78-0696, belonging to the 926th TFG, bears its tusks at the enemy. *Campbell*

This extremely agitated canine mimics the fire power of this A-10A. The view affords a clear look at that power. *Campbell*

Panther Princess, serial 78-594, an A-10A of the 353rd TFS at Myrtle Beach AFB, S.C. *James*

Tiger Meet

In the United States we have a weapons competition at Nellis AFB Nevada called William Tell — another is called Gunsmoke. In Europe the NATO forces have their equal in Tiger Meet. This and following aircraft from our NATO allies pay a small tribute to the noble competition. Much beauty and the artist's skill is richly displayed here in what is truly the essence of aircraft art.

A CF-104C of the RCAF at Sollingen in 1976, serial 104756, is seen in total tiger camo while assigned to the 439th Squadron. The tiger is somewhat humorous in its attempt to be menacing. *KAHS*

On this RCAF F-104 "Starfighter" in Tiger Meet camo the artist was required to omit painting the nose cone due to internal radar. *KAHS*

This F-16A, serial FA-94, of the 31st Squadron, is at RAF Fairford, July 1991. The bold tail number depicting the squadron has an interesting contrast to the subdued grey on charcoal tiger camo, as well as the bright full color Tiger Meet camo of the forward section of this beautifully painted fighter. *James*

Where as this is only a tiger insignia the label is interesting in the fact that it is being carried on a Mig-29, serial 32356, assigned to CZ 11 Fighter Regiment, a rare guest at RAF Fairford. *James*

This Italian built Fiat G-91R, serial 5452, assigned to the 301 Esq, displays a grim set of teeth. Photo at RAF Fairford. *James*

This Puma HC.1, of the Royal Air Force, serial XW224, assigned to the 230th squadron, is at RAF Fairford. This Puma lives up to its name with the colorful rendition of the tiger on the rotor boom. *James*

Where the U.S. Navy isn't as keen on nose art as the Air Force, we have a nice example of what they can do when allowed in **Killer Whale,** an EA-3B, serial 146454, assigned to VQ-2 with the nose #004. This tanker at RAF Fairford in July 1991 shows an example of the spirit of the crew and their esteem. *James*

More Tiger Meet at RAF Fairford, 1991. This Mirage F.1C not only carries a beautiful tiger camouflage but the tiger head insignia of 162nd Squadron. *James*

This F-16A, serial J-012, belongs to the 313th Squadron of the Czech Air Force. This photo was taken at RAF Fairford, England in 1991 and carries a well done air brushing of the Bengal Tiger. *James*

This Italian F-104 is assigned to the 53rd Stormo (squadron) serial, 53-04. Photo taken at RAF Fairford. *James*

This F-111E, serial 68-0049, U.S. Tiger Meet participant, is assigned to the 20th TFW, RAF Fairford. *James*

Mary Rose, a Jaguar GR1A, serial X2356, belonged to the 6th Squadron, RAF, Fairford. *James*

Lucky Lou, a Victor, K-2, serial XM717, belonged to the 55th Squadron, RAF, Mildenhall. *James*

One Bad Bitch, an RC-12D, serial 80-23373, belonged to the RAF, Mildenhall. *James*

RAF

Sweet Sue was on a Victor, K-2, serial XH671, belonging to the 55th Squadron, RAF, Fairford. *James*

This caped figure was on an EP-3E, serial 157320, assigned to the RAF, Fairford. *James*

The art, **Hello Sailor Caroline,** was found on a Buccaneer, S2B, serial XX885, belonging to the RAF, Fairford. *James*

Sabre One, an F-16C, serial 84-1315, belonged to the 50th TFW, RAF, Bentwaters. *James*

This fire breathing dragon was on a Tornado, GR1, mm 7040, 36-35, belonging to the RAF, and stationed at Bentwaters. *James*

This close-up of **Lucky Lou** shows the number of refueling missions flown by the aircraft as marked by gas pumps. *James*

This stylized Arabian bat was on the EP-3E, serial 157320, **Evelyn.** Note the radar missions flown by this aircraft. RAF, Fairford. *James*

Decorative Ordnance and Pods

This travel pod, carrying the name **Jersey Devils,** was on an F-16A, serial 80-0618, belonging to the 119th FIS, New Jersey ANG. *James*

S/Sgt Ricky Abbott and T/Sgt Marty Lochman are responsible for the art found on the travel pod belonging to the 507th Fighter Group (AF RES) Commander, Lt.Col. Robert E. Lytle. The 507th FG, 465th TFS is based at Tinker AFB, Oklahoma City. Note the F-16, Falcon trailing the stars and stripes along the side of the pod. *Curry*

In keeping with the medical terminology, surgical bombing, used during Operation Desert Storm, is the message **This Wont Hurt 1 Bit** followed by **Don't Worry Be Happy** found on this bomb also belonging to the 4th TFS. *Curry*

This photo shows the second message on the above bomb more clearly. *Curry*

This bomb carrying the message **Pucker Up** with a pair of hot lips also belonged to the 4th TFS. *Curry*

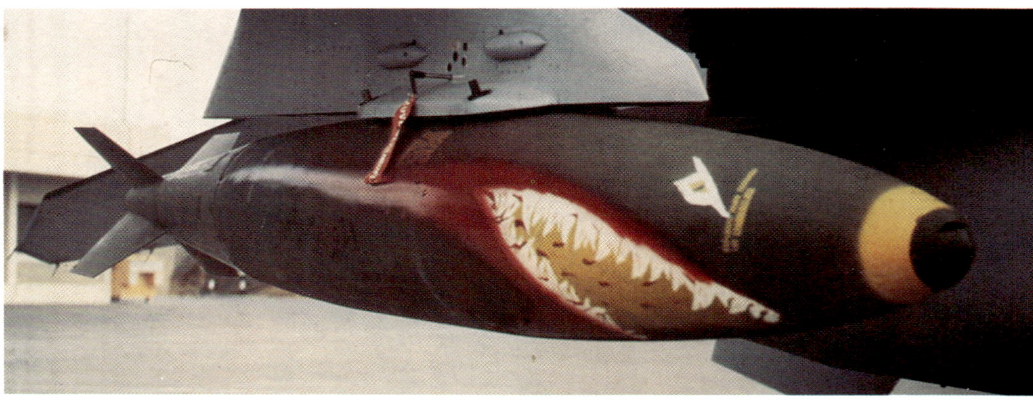

This photo shows an adaptation of the shark mouth design, first made famous by the Flying Tigers before America's entrance into WWII. This ordinance also belonged to the 4th TFS. *Curry*

From an American jingle for the sale of Budweiser comes the message, **"Saddam For All You Do This Ones 4-U"** followed by **Hello!!** These messages were from members of the 4th TFS. *Curry*

The 1960s era peace symbol used by those opposing the Vietnam War decorated this ordinance to be used in a more popular military operation. It carried the message **Peace You Had Your Chance!** *Curry*

As in wars before, the weapons and ordinance used during Desert Storm carried messages to the enemy. This more modern war allowed for a newer form of applying those messages as seen in this photo of a crew member applying the word Iraq with a can of spray paint. This ordinance was carried by an F-16 belonging to the 4th TFS out of Hill AFB. *Curry*

F-4

This F-4B, #212, serial 150632, is assigned to Fighter Squadron 111 at Miramar, California. This aircraft, assigned to the carrier Coral Sea, is dressed out in the color scheme of the 1970s with the shark mouth and upturned eyes. *Gregory*

This shark mouth design is on an F-4E, serial 68-0374, belonging to the 110th TFS, MO ANG. Pictured 23 September 1988, St. Louis, Missouri. *James*

Dragon Slayer featured a fire breathing dragon of old with the chosen weapon of today, a missile, piercing his neck. This F-4D is another of the 507th TFG aircraft. *Campbell*

The Mayberry Express was on an F-4, serial 65-0590, belonging to the Kansas ANG. This photo was taken 23 March 1986, McConnell AFB. *KAHS*

Kansas Crop Duster, an F-4, serial 65-0798, belonged to the Kansas ANG, stationed at McConnell AFB. *KAHS*

Tell Me Twice was on an F-4D belonging to the 507th TFG, Tinker AFB, Oklahoma City. *Campbell*

PHANTOM FLASHERS, the art on this Phantom II, serial 67-685, displays a bit of the western gunslinger. Pictured at Tinker AFB, Oklahoma City, it bears the colors of the Oklahoma State University "Cowboys." *James*

This current version of **Dragon Lady** is on an F-4, serial 66-484. *James*

Blending the early frontier with the present is the F-4, serial 63-565, belonging to the 122 TFW, **City of Fort Wayne.** *James*

The brave little mouse faces the attacking eagle with the aid of a club hidden behind his back on the F-4C, serial 63-7534, **Defiance II,** belonging to the MI ANG. This photo was taken at Selfridge, 5 May 1980. *KAHS*

This Bull was found on the intake panel of an F-4, serial 66-570. *James*

Left: This F-4D, serial 66-242, carried two names **Animal** and **Wonder Jet.** This aircraft belonged to the Kansas ANG. *KAHS*

Right: **Naughty Lady,** an F-4, serial 65-772, belonged to the Kansas ANG. *KAHS*

Hillbilly Slick is seen on the RF-4C, serial 65-0870, belonging to the 11th TRS based at Udorn, Thailand at the RTAFB. *KAHS*

Lil' Bee decorated the RF-4C, serial 65-0908, belonging to the 11th TRS in Udorn, Thailand. *KAHS*

The RF-4C, serial 65-912A, was named **The Joyce Elaine.** This photo of the 11th TRS Phantom was taken in 1969 at RTAFB where it was stationed. *KAHS*

This patch-work puppy was found on the RF-4C, **Ol Bullet,** serial 64-1039, piloted by Jack Ferguson. The Navigator was Barry Johnson. The aircraft was among those serving at RTAFB. *KAHS*

"Hey Bud" was found on the RF-4C, serial 65-0908, belonging to the 11th TRS, Udorn, RTAFB. This photo was taken October 1969. *KAHS*

Walking away from his bombed-out dog house is **Snoopy** as seen on this RF-4C Phantom belonging to the 11th TRS and piloted by Larry Krotz with Dick Bower as Navigator. Over the smoking house are the words, "War's Hell." *KAHS*

Crazy Horse, an RF-4C, was one of the aircraft belonging to the 173rd TRS, Nebraska ANG. *James*

Miss Piggy was found on the nose gear door of an F-4C, serial 63-638, belonging to the 182nd TFS, Texas ANG. *James*

Lips II was the name given to another of the F-4Ds belonging to the Kansas ANG. It was serial 65-0598. *KAHS*

The art on the F-4C, serial 64-0707, **don't mess with the kid,** centered around Bugs Bunny. This aircraft belonged to the MI ANG. It had its picture taken at RAF Mildenhall. *James*

This form of aircraft decoration was seen during WWII when some pilots and crews put paintings or photos in the windows of photo recon aircraft. This photo appears to be from a current magazine. It was seen on an RF4B, serial 153092. *James*

This picture of the **Tasmanian Devil** was found on a F-4D belonging to the 127th TFS, Kansas ANG. *KAHS*

This missile-carrying camel was seen on the F-4D, serial 66-0229, belonging to the Kansas ANG. *KAHS*

Wally Gator is on a fishing trip but along with his pole he is also carrying a couple of wrenches. This RF-4C carried the serial 65-0917. *James*

Left The F-4, serial 66-816, has used its serial number to make up its full house which consisted of sixes and eights. **Full House** belonged to the 704th TFS. *KAHS*

Right This ornery character on **Yosemite Sam II** is familiar to most of us. He is seen on this Kansas ANG F-4D, serial 65-705, along with the words, "Git Them Varmits." *KAHS*

Hanger Queenie, an RF-4C, serial 68-0605, was assigned to the 190th TRS, Indiana ANG. *James*

Widow Maker, an F-4D, serial 65-0614, belonged to the 127th TFS, Kansas ANG. *KAHS*

This Kansas ANG F-4, serial 65-0687, was called **The Apple Flyer.** *KAHS*

Lady Luck, an F-4D, serial 65-711, belonged to Kansas ANG. *KAHS*

In honor of the Star Trek fans, this F-4D was named **Enterprise.** Under the name it carried the NCC 1701 from the star ship and the familiar quote, **"Beam me up Scotty!"** was beside the name. *James*

The name **Baby Doll** was carried by the F-4D, serial 65-0660, belonging to the Kansas ANG, McConnell AFB. *KAHS*

G-Wiz was the name accompanying this caricature of the F-4 showing a tail code of SH 548. The aircraft is shown with blood shot eyes and muttering the words, "9.8 Gs-s-s-s." The art was signed, Ken "84." *Bacon*

This beloved Disney character who taught us that wishes could come true, was seen on the landing gear door of this F-4. *James*

This little armadillo, also known as a Texas turkey, was on an F-4, serial 64-0699. *James*

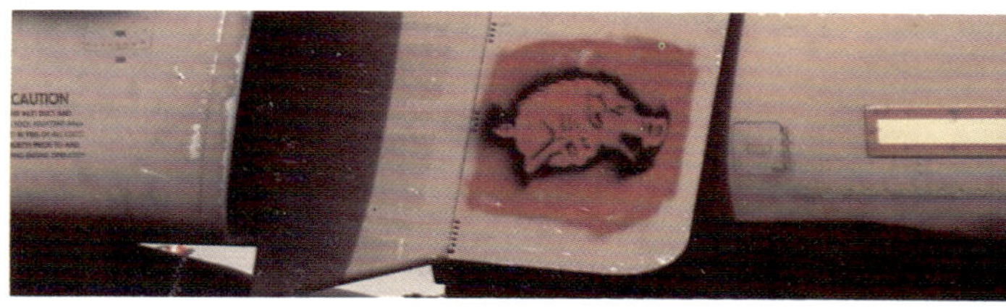

This running razor back was on an F-4, serial 64-0879. *James*

Rolling Thunder, an F-4D mini-gun pod, is on an aircraft assigned to the Kansas ANG at McConnell AFB, Kansas. Many units applied names and art to the gun pod just as to the aircraft. *Davis*

The words **The Wreckin Crew** are in the shape of a wrecking ball and it appears to be hanging by a chain. Inside the circle is a pair of crossed mallets. This art was found on an RF-4C belonging to the 56th TFW at Korat AFB. *KAHS*

'UA'U KANI, serial 63-491, is assigned to the 199th TFS in the Hawaii ANG which was later redesignated the 154th Composite Group. This F-4C is proud of its heritage and home state. *James*

This art honors Lt.Col. Wayne Yarolem of the 181st TFG for 5000 hours flown from July 1967 to April 1985. It was on an F-4, serial 63-437. *James*

The interesting shark mouth on this RF-4C Phantom II belongs to the Nevada ANG. It is attending an open house at Nellis AFB in mid 1990. The blood stained teeth would have you believe the aircraft is still hungry. *Truax*

This Phantom is in a lot better mood compared to many of the sharks teeth we have encountered. Seen in the shelters which are commonplace to England and Germany, as well as other NATO countries it is difficult to determine its exact location. *Watts*

The tiger on the nose of this F-4E, serial 68-0533, belonging to the 141st TFS, shows what can be done with camouflage by reversing colors, dark on light and light on dark. This aircraft belonged to the New Jersey ANG. *James*

This F-4E, serial 68-305, belonging to the 43rd TFS, Elmendorf AFB, Alaska, is in what seems to be a rather enraged state. She is seen here at Tyndal AFB on 18 November 1976 attending the annual William Tell fighter competition. *KAHS*

Blackbird, an F-4J Phantom, serial 153783, was assigned to VX-4 at Point Magu Naval Air Station. The reader will notice the bands of azure blue with stars on wing tips as well as the "Playboy Bunny" on the vertical. *Que*

This shot at Edwards ABF of an YF-4C, shows the emblem for the SFCS fly by wire test experiments. This would prove to be invaluable in future generations of aircraft. *KAHS*

Spirit of America, an RF-4, bears an interesting paint scheme, the crossed American flags on the vertical display the pride in country, as well as the traditional U.S. Marine Esprit De Corps. The anti-glare panel runs the length of the spine to the radio antenna. *KAHS*

In examining the F-4N, serial 153012, we see an aging Phantom belonging to VF-111. This particular aircraft was assigned to the carrier USS Franklin D. Roosevelt. We have what might be referred to as one last look due to this aircraft's condition and location seen here at Davis-Montham AFB, AZ. It is also noteworthy that the color slashes on the vertical would indicate that this aircraft was a CAG (Commander Air Group) bird. *Fritz*

F-4D Phantom **North Dakota Centennial,** serial 66-7498, of the 119th TFG. This beautiful Phantom II is a commemorative aircraft. The "Happy Hooligans" is the nickname given to the North Dakota ANG. This aircraft carries the state seal on the undersurface of the fuselage and wing. *Hill*

Eagle 1, an F-4N, assigned to VX-4, exhibits the work of the US Navy in the very artistic way in which they dressed-up their Bicentennial aircraft, ships which were created to celebrate our country's 200th year of freedom. *KAHS*

Skunk Works

Shark II, tail art, is on an SR-71, Black Bird, serial 17960, belonging to the 9th SRW. The Black Bird, by definition, does not lend itself readily to art. Although this is subdued art it does make its point. This photo was taken at Beale AFB, California, November 1988, during open house. *Veronico*

The SR-71, serial 17976, also has subdued art on its tail. This one showing the head of a tiger. The artist signed his work with the single name Ward. *Veronico*

This cat is on the U-2R, serial 68-10336, belonging to the 9th SRW. The photo was taken January 1980, at Hickam AFB. *KAHS*

With Operation Desert Storm behind us now the F-117A demonstrated that the stealth concept would in fact work, and that combat operations would indeed surpass all expectations in regards to projected losses. A total of fifty-nine aircraft were procured having lost only two aircraft during a mid-air mishap during test phase at Edwards AFB. The Skunk Works at Lockheed certainly earned their spurs with this dynamic creation. It is necessary to explain that the art on all F-117A's was applied inside the weapons bays on the bomb bay door. This was due to the nature of stealth technology and the ability of radars to get a signature just from the paint used for the art. This rare shot of an F-117A coupling to the boom of its mother tanker was taken during Operation Desert Storm. *Curry*

The TR-1A/U-2, serial 80-1099, belonged to the 95th RS. The painting on the tail of this aircraft depicts popular comic book character Calvin with his visor and spy camera. The unique lightning bolt on his T-shirt reveals the sinister and macabre nature of most of the aircraft which originated at Lockheed's famous "Skunk Works." Picture taken at RAF Fairford 20 July 1991. *James*

Above: **Midnight Reaper,** an F-117A, a/c #839. Many of the operations flown by F-117A's were flown at night, however, not all were deployed during the witching hours. The artist chose to create a sinister demon harvesting its quarry at Midnight. *Campbell*

Above left: **Habu II,** an F-117A, a/c #837. The aviation enthusiast will recall that Habu, the SR-71 Blackbird's nickname, was applied to another Lockheed Skunk Works project, Habu II seen here prepared to inflict serious pain or injury. *Campbell*

Left: This rather grisly bit of art found on the F-117A, a/c #813, **The Toxic Avenger,** is somewhat symbolic of the effect on human tissues after the use of chemical warfare. The most probable explanation for this art was the evident fear that the Iraqi military would employ the use of chemical warfare agents. *Campbell*

The art on this F-117A, Stealth Fighter, aircraft #798, specifies its affiliation with the 415th TFS. Named **Aces and Eights,** it shows a full house consisting of just that. Note the Ace of Spades bears the image of the Stealth in place of the usual spade. *Campbell*

Left: This F-117A, a/c #836, **Christine,** reflects the works of Steven King and his flair for the bizarre and unholy, as this art was inspired by the killer Chevy in the movie "Christine." *Campbell*

The F-117A, a/c #808, **Thor,** named for the God of Thunder is depicted here aggressively leading the attack. It is to the credit of the designers and pilots that no F-117A's were lost in Desert Storm. *Campbell*

Above right: This silhouette of the F-117A, a/c #801, with the Perpetrator reclined on the spine of the aircraft holding a fused bomb ready to make a delivery, was appropriately named, **Perpetrator.** *Campbell*

Something Wicked, an F-117A, a/c #806. Ray Bradbury's literary work is reflected in the art on this Stealth Fighter. The name was taken from the book and movie "Something Wicked, This Way Comes." It was the story of sinister traveling carnival personalities which arrived at night to work their evil ways on the unsuspecting townsfolk. *Campbell*

The Dragon, an F-117A, a/c #835. The Dragon symbol for Detachment 1 of the 57th Fighter Weapons Wing at Tonopah adorns the art in this photo. Note the dragon's footprints. *Campbell*

Final Verdict, an F-117A, a/c #814. This winged female is perched ready to act on the final verdict as soon as the scales tip their decision. *Campbell*

War Pig, the F-117A, a/c #786, carried the image of an angry Warthog in camouflage pants with weapons at the ready in both hands. Note the aircraft number 786 on the jersey. *Campbell*

Delta Dawn, an F-117A, a/c #794, got its name from the song "Delta Dawn." This is certainly not a faded rose from days gone by. The art enhances the artists appreciation of beauty. *Campbell*

Named for a popular movie which showed a women out of control is the F-117A, a/c #796, **Fatal Attraction.** The Femme Fatale seen here enjoying the sweet smell of a rose, is prepared to deliver a fatal blow with her tomahawk. *Campbell*

Wiley E. Coyote's Tritonal Express, an F-117A, a/c #793. Wiley seen standing beside a paveway smart bomb. The current art, like its earlier counterpart, also often focuses on cartoon characters. *Campbell*

This sword bearing heroine, clearly intent on doing combat, openly displays our pride and devotion to duty. This art was, as with all the art seen on the Stealth Fighters, inside the weapons bay. This being on the F-117A, a/c #841, **Mystic Warrior.** *Campbell*

Magic Hammer, an F-117A, a/c #838. One of Thor's children seen here with the hammer emitting lightning and thunder. The F-117As certainly did a lot of that and much more. *Campbell*

Nachtfalke, an F-117A, a/c #821. The painting seen here of Donald Duck was seen in World War II on a B-24 of the European Theatre of Operations, with the trailer, "Back to the Sack." The translated explanation of NACHTFALKE is German for Night Hawk. As was mentioned before the F-117A's flew many of their attack sorties at night. *Campbell*

Lone Wolf, an F-117A, a/c #816. The artist, pilot or creator of this art could be expressing how alone one may feel while flying a mission in an aircraft which renders itself invisible to radar. *Campbell*

Double Down, an F-117A, a/c #811. Pictured here we clearly see a double, in the ace of spades we see the number 37, representative of the 37th Tactical Fighter Wing, and the name Las Vegas for the approximate location of the Tonopah test range in Nevada. *Campbell*

Lazy Ace, an F-117A, a/c #791. A Snoozing pilot seen here in a World War I vintage aircraft depict the comfort the pilot feels in the confines of this aircraft. *Campbell*

F-15, F-101, F-106, F-111

F-106A, serial 59-0043, belonging to the 177th FIG, New Jersey ANG.

Hawk One Canada, an CF-101B, serial 101012, belonged to the 409th Squadron, RCAF. This aircraft performed a fly by in honor of Queen Elizabeth's 2nd Silver Jubilee Celebration during her visit to Canada. Picture taken 10 September 1977. *KAHS*

This F-15C, carrying the name **Wolfhounds,** was piloted by Col. Lee Alton, of the 32nd TFS. *Bacon*

This F-15C, serial 79-0032, also from the 32nd TFS, bears the name **Wolfhounds** but has a more subdued art. It was based at RAF Bentwaters. *James*

Maloney's Pony, an F-15A, was piloted by Lt. Chuck Coghlin. *James*

Gulf Spirit, an F-15, serial 75-069, shows a patriotic piece of art which includes the state of Florida. *James*

This royal hog was found on the F-101, serial 70-412, belonging to the 123rd FIS. The Voodoo named **The Queen Hog** was photographed 4 October 1978. *Isham, via Bacon*

The art on this F-15 represented and was named for the **City of Alamogordo,** New Mexico. *Bacon*

This not too intimidating aberration was on the F-101B named **The Gray Ghost.** *KAHS*

This view of the F-106A, serial 59-0043, shows the shark mouth and the 177th FIG insignia, **The Spirit of Atlantic City.** *James*

This RF-101, Voodoo, bears the insignia of the Flight Test Facility, Edwards AFB, California. *James*

This shot and the one above left and below are of the F-106, serial 59-0043, pictured at the top of page 44. These three photos were taken at Tinker AFB on the trip to Davis-Montham AFB. *James*

On this side is the Jersey Devil of the 177th FIG NJ ANG with the dates 1972 through 1988. On the nose is a list of all the Fighter Intercepter Squadrons of the 177th FIG. Down the fuselage are the names of many crew members. *James*

This shots reveals the 1984 William Tell competition award and a few more names. *James*

June Nite, was the name given to this F-111, serial 680077. *James*

Miss Liberty II, an F-111F, serial 70-2390, was assigned to the 48th TFW. This aircraft was at RAF Mildenhall. *James*

Liberator II, an F-111, serial 80-287, shows a painting of a WWII B-24. The explanation for the art is written next to it and reads: Named in tribute to the Eighth Air Force men who flew and fought over Europe in the Consolidated B-24 Liberator 11 Sep 1942 - 9 July 1945. *James*

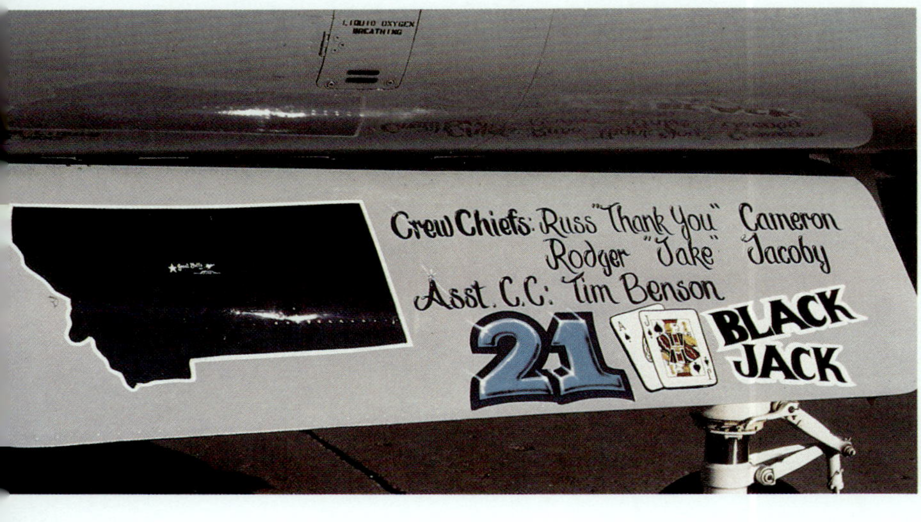

This landing gear door art **21 Black Jack** was on an F-106A, serial 57-2530, assigned to the 120th FIG. *James*

KC-10, KC-130, KC-135

BT Express, was the name given this KC-10, serial 84-0185. *James*

Ace of Spades was found on a KC-10A, serial 84-0189. *James*

Haul On Call also describes the duty preformed by this C-130E, serial 64-0542, belonging to the 317th TAW, Pope AFB, Louisiana. Photo taken 27 May 1990 at RAF Mildenhall. *James*

Named for its service, the KC-130, serial 148895, **Hose Monster** was used as a refueling tanker by VR-22. Photographed at RAF Woodbridge 22 February 1990. *James*

Rollin Thunder was on the EC-135A, serial 61-0262. *Link*

This Boeing 135 bears the nose art of Alley-Oop. The Squadron designation is unknown. *Conger*

Straight out of WWII comes this nose art named **Command Decision.** This time it is on a KC-135R, serial 59-1478. *Link*

"Ultimate Warrior" carried the painting of a proud American Indian. This KC-135R, serial 63-8023, served with the 305th ARW. *James*

Another proud American Eagle graced the nose of this KC-135, serial 63-8054. This photo was taken at Tinker AFB, Oklahoma. *Campbell*

The KC-135, **Kukai Maru,** serial 1512, belonged to the 452nd Air Refueling Wing. *Bacon*

Above left This shot of the KC-135 **Kukai Maru** shows the mission markers for its service during Desert Shield, 1990. *Bacon*

Nordik Warrior, painted by Lee Jacobson was on the KC-135A, serial 56-3647, belonging to the 410th BW, RAF, Fairford. Picture was taken 22 July 1989. *James*

This very American symbol was found on a KC-135A, serial 52-3498, proudly named **Arkansas Eagle.** *Link*

Right That "Wascally Wabbit" Bugs Bunny was on the nose of the KC-135R, serial 57-1439, **The Old Grey Hare.** Next to the name is written, "Dedicated to the memory of Hector Jimerez Jr. 22 Jan 1968 to 26 May 1991." Photo taken at Tinker AFB, Oklahoma. *Link*

A new generation of characters is being seen on some of the current aircraft. This one is titled **Big Byrd.** The large yellow bird was on a KC-135E, serial 60-0372. It was named for the crew chief, WG-13 Byrd. This photo was taken at Tinker AFB, Oklahoma. *Link*

Speedie Gee shows a western desperado riding a winged mule. Pictured at Tinker AFB, Oklahoma. *Link*

The KC-135R, serial 63-8008, was named **Flying Dutchman.** It was assigned to the 19th ARW. *Link*

Flying Free was on a KC-135. *Hill*

Eight Ball, serial 63-8000, was the name given to the KC-135A belonging to the 22nd ARW. Picture taken 20 September 1988. Offutt AFB, Nebraska. *James*

Miscellaneous Aircraft

This colorful T-38A of the US Navy, assigned to China Lake test range, carries the serial 1596, as well as the colors of our nation's great flag. The stars and stripes design could conceivably classify this aircraft as a bicentennial aircraft even without the numerical "76" notation. *Campbell*

Here we see an A-4M Aggressor, serial 160022, assigned to Marine Attack Squadron 311. On the vertical is an all too familiar friend from the silver screen, a transformed Gremlin. The aviators have had the belief almost since the beginning of flight that the little creatures known as gremlins were the cause of all little glitches in the aircraft's performance. *Truax*

This TA-4F Skyhawk, serial 153674, assigned to the operational test and evaluation force (VX-4) "Evaluators" at Point Mugu bears the grimacing shark's mouth of a hungry aggressor. This photo was taken in November 1975. *Campbell*

Lady Jessie, serial 155018, was an A-4F assigned to Attack Squadron 164 at NAS Lemoore, California. It carries the stylized flashes as well as the lettering to match. *Copeland*

The TA-4J, serial 153463, was assigned to the Naval Air Reserve Unit. The red white and blue is also displayed in the overall paint scheme here. *KAHS*

This A-4M was assigned to the Marine Air Attack Squadron 214, "The Black Sheep", founded by the world famous ace and fighter pilot Gregory "Pappy" Boyington. During World War II fighter squadrons were referred to as FMFs for the US Marines. This aircraft, serial 160044, is piloted by Lt.Col. Jim "Eagle" Underwood. The squadron insignia, the Ram, can clearly be seen here at this sitting at Andrews AFB in October 1978. *Campbell*

This Bicentennial TA-4J, serial 154290, was caught on the ramp at Naval Air Station Miramar "Fighter Town" in Oct 1975. The official bicentennial seal is plain on the mid-fuselage area of this aircraft as well as beautiful trim and piping. *Copeland*

F-106A, serial 59-0076 was assigned to the 49th Fighter Interceptor Squadron at Griffiss AFB. This image shows the squadron patch centered over the unit emblem, the eagle. The flag and serial 1790076 on the vertical would indicate it to be a bicentennial bird. The 49th Fighter Squadron had a very impressive career from World War II up to its retirement several years ago. *James*

The C-54 bearing the number 76 pictured here is serving with the US Forestry Service as a borate bomber. It is serial N76AU. The pride of country is seen here in the red, white and blue of the fuselage and vertical. Seen at Windslow, Arizona in May 1978. This aircraft, as well as her brothers, fly in low and drop fire retardant materials on active forest fires. *KAHS*

City of Jacksonville. We find two separate views of this beautifully done F-106A serial 58-0760. The red white and blue as well as the field of stars indicate the patriotism and spirit for the bicentennial celebration this aircraft represents. Assigned to the 159th Fighter Interceptor Squadron, Florida ANG. *Campbell*

This Bicentennial T-39, assigned to Training squadron 10, was serial 150980. The art would express the desire to show the national seal and our national bird "The Bald Eagle." This aircraft was piloted by Capt. J. Finney. *Campbell*

Above left: This C-117D, Gooney Bird, serial 17156, civilian registry N722NR, displays an awkward and somewhat ugly Gooney Bird with flight helmet and roller skates, equipment necessary to build up take off speed. Photo was taken at NAS China Lake in 1989. This aircraft provides an accurate example of current nose art on a day-glow background. *James*

Left: The bite of the A-4 Skyhawk is seen here with the last bomb of the Vietnam war from the standpoint of this particular air wing. The red, white and blue would certainly attest to the love of country and respect for the flag. *Miller via Pickett*

Left: The T-2C **Spirit of America** was another bicentennial aircraft. This one, assigned to Training Squadron 25 at Beeville, Texas, tells its visitors to "Be someone special" a recruitment logo to be sure. Serial 157057 carries the official bicentennial seal on the upper vertical with the number 76 plainly visible for effect. The red, white and blue add a nice effect to the overall paint scheme of this aircraft. The photo was taken at NAS Atlanta in 1978. *KAHS*

Rosineu Bomber, pronounced rosy new, a C-54, serial 050557, sits in the half round hanger at Templehof Airport in Germany. This photo was taken in 1982 but in 1945-1946 many cargo aircraft such as this flew in food and supplies to the Germans in the Berlin Airlift. *Watts*

Spirit of New Mexico, serial 65-10367. This T-38A is assigned to the Air Force Reserves at Holloman AFB, New Mexico, in the 479th TFW. In the upper right corner we see the Indian symbol for the state as well as the state bird, the roadrunner at the bottom. *Reeves*

City of Alamogordo, an AT-38B, serial 71-4842, also based at Holloman AFB, carries a scenic painting incorporating the Indian symbol for the state, the sun and the mountains as well as two T-38s to symbolize their pride. This aircraft belongs to the 479th TFW. *James*

Air Guard Number 1 was the name of this KC-97L of the 197th Air Refueling Squadron, 161st Air Refueling Group, Phoenix ANG Arizona. The aircraft, serial 53-0243, carries her art in the traditional and patriotic red, white and blue. *Campbell*

This DC-9, civilian registry N950PB, is the personal aircraft of Hugh Hefner and the Playboy Club International. The bunny on the vertical would certainly sum up what nose art is all about. *Campbell*

This A-6E, serial 155632, was assigned to Marine Attack Squadron 224. The squadron insignia of the tiger coming through a brick wall as seen here on the vertical reflects the attitude of most Intruder/Prowler crews. The A-6 series of aircraft were not, at best, fast aircraft, but they delivered one hell of a lot of devastation, from their first use in Vietnam, their mission with VA-75 to Libya to bomb Kahdafi, to their most recent assaults on Baghdad. The A-6s have won a place in the hearts of those who crewed her. *James*

TAZ, a T-2C, at Beeville, Texas, serial 15-8138, bears a small but nicely done Tasmanian Devil. Way to go Navy. *James*

Tiny Tim, tail code TT, carrying a full load of bombs, sits in the Search Air Rescue slot. This aircraft would become airborne at only a few minutes notice to fly in and interfere with the capture of a downed airman using cannons, and bombs to dissuade the Viet Cong from their quarry. *Campbell*

Magnet-Ass, A-1J Skyraider. Many of the "Sandys" as the Air Force affectionately nicknamed this fine aircraft. The Sandy delivered as large of a bomb load as did the B-17 Flying Fortress of World War II and flew many interdiction missions in N Vietnam. *Campbell*

AV-8B Harrier, piloted by Capt. R. Regan, call sign "Nightmare", has a camel on the scoreboard and an angry bee with telescope and bomb in her clutches. This is another Desert Storm veteran. *James*

AV-8B, another view of the Harrier piloted by R. Regan this time we view the art work of Angel in reclining position holding a little airplane. Serial 162722. Photo taken at Tinker AFB, Oklahoma City. *James*

SAP SUCKING 80, a Martin built B-57 Canberra bomber, serial 53-3856, carries an interesting overall black paint scheme with the stencil type art work of the Bald Eagle. This aircraft was assigned to the 134 DSES(ANG) 158 DSEG at Burlington, Vermont in 1980. The overall black paint would indicate its mission duties were many times night missions. *Watts*

TF-10B Savage, serial 124630, chickbird, seen here while on static display at Vance AFB, Enid, Oklahoma. This aircraft used for weapons delivery operations in New Mexico and Arizona spotting artillery. *Watts*

Eyes of the Fleet was the name given to this RF-8A assigned to VFP-63. Note the aggressive look in the eyes painted mid section on the aircraft in this photo taken in June of 1970. This aircraft did photographic recon missions while aboard the USS John F. Kennedy during the Vietnam conflict. *James*

This TF-104B, serial 0-63722, carries the shark mouth unusual to this type and time of aircraft. This two seat configuration was used for training purposes. *Watts*

OV-10A, This U.S. Marine "Bronco" carries the hornet on the nose of this fast but effective ground support aircraft. Navy & Marine Corps aircraft are not known for nose art due to regulations and wide spread use of the airplanes so it is certainly a treat to see pieces of it from time to time. *James*

Northrop's YF-17. This aircraft carries on the nose its name Cobra. This rare prototype aircraft was the competitor for the McDonnell Douglas Hornet. Where only a few were manufactured it was truly a beautiful aircraft. This one piloted by Hank Ghouteau. *KAHS*

Pink Panther, an AT-28, was a member of the Laotian Air Force. These small but durable aircraft flew forward warning and fire suppression missions out of Udorn, Thailand during the Vietnam War. *Campbell*

These two Lockheed views of this early Korean War fighter vividly display the squadron insignia of the 68th Fighter Interceptor Squadron, "Lightning Lancers." Photo of parked aircraft is serial 15355, while the in flight shot reveals 15346 as well as the smooth line of the F-94. *Spry*

We see a very dangerous looking shark mouth here with sidewinder missile on the right fuselage rail of this RF-8, assigned to VF-111, aboard the US Shangra-La. This photo was taken from inside the wingman's F-8. Serial 148677. *KAHS*

This RF-8 Crusader is a classic example of the inspiration of art by the shipboard genius. Nose art wasn't, for the most part, dress-of-the-day, whereas adorning the tail or vertical didn't draw too much negative feedback. This F-8, serial 146895, was assigned to the USS Coral Sea, VFP-63 Detachment 3. The P after the VF (fighter squadron) identifies the aircraft as a photo recon F-8. *James*

F-8D, serial 147055, was piloted by Lt. Chuck Scott of VF-111 aboard the Shangri-La. The significant art on this "Sundowner" is the vicious set of sharks teeth backed up in reality by the menacing sidewinder missile on the rail. *James*

F-8F Crusader, serial 145562, was assigned to Marine Fighter Squadron 321. This colorful F-8 is natural gull gray with a top fuselage of gloss black speckled with a field of white stars as well as black with stars on the lower ventral fins. *James*

This F-89 Scorpion, serial 0-32594, belonging to the 119th TFG, is pictured in 1975 at what appears to be an open house in Fargo, N. Dakota. Note **The Happy Hooligans** logo on the wing tip pods as well as the ANG seal under the horizontal slab. *James*

Another **Happy Hooligans.** This being on an F-101B Voodoo, serial 70252, belonging to 178 FIS, and seen at Offutt AFB. The Hooligan's sash on the vertical shows the lite touch of art common on the F-101s and F-4Ds. *Hill*

F-105

This shark mouth F-105G, serial 62-4425, belonged to the Georgia ANG. It also carried a name on intake. *KAHS*

The FREEK, an F-105G, serial 62-4442, was assigned to the 17th Wild Weasel Squadron at Korat, Thailand. Photo taken in February 1973. Note the blood dripping from the somewhat gruesome fang of this Thunderchief. *Campbell*

This shark mouth was found on an F-105G stationed at Korat AB, Thailand. *KAHS*

Believe it or not, this is not art from Desert Storm. This F-105D, serial 62-4299, was assigned to the 466th TFS, 508th TFG. This photo of **Desert Fox** was taken 2 April 1983 at Nellis AFB, Nevada. *Bacon*

This "Old West" motif was found on the F-105D, serial 61-0164, **Golden Gun.** This was also one of the aircraft of the 149th TFS. *Kaston, via Bacon*

This strange combination of lion and tiger was found on the F-105D, **The Liger,** serial 61-355, assigned to the Air Base at Davis-Montham in Arizona. *Bacon*

the Hun's Hammer, an F-105D, serial 59-1731, belonged to the 149th TFS. *Kaston, via Bacon*

This little red devil was found on the lower fuselage of the F-105D, serial 62-4228, **Silver Tongue "Devil"** belonging to the 466th TFS, 508th TFG. The photo was taken 8 May 1983 at Marine Corps Air Station, El Toro, California. *Bacon*

This painting of **Muttley The Flying Dog** was on the F-105G, serial 63-8291, which flew with the 17th WWS (Wild Weasle Squadron). This photo was taken in Krat AB, Thailand, February 1973. *KAHS*

This close-up of the F-105 on the top of the opposite page, serial 62-4425, shows the name which in Thai letters spells Kloyjai, which was the name of the pilot's wife. The pilot was Capt. Jim Boyd. *KAHS*

This Roman Gladiator is giving tips on how to knock missiles out of the sky. Named **Do It With . . . Finesse,** is the F-105, serial 63-362, belonging to the Virginia ANG. *KAHS*

For those who watch the stars, we have **Aquarius** on an F-105D, serial 60-488. This aircraft flew with the 44th TFS, 355th TFW. The photo was taken October, 1970. *James*

Jinkin Josie was the art on the F-105F, serial 63-8301, belonging to the 357th TFS. This art is reminiscent of that found on aircraft of WWII. *KAHS*

The Dirty Duck was on an F-105F, serial 63-8365A, which was stationed at Hill AFB, Utah. *James*

The F-105F, serial 62-4413, **Flying Anvil,** belonged to the Virginia ANG. *KAHS*

"**The Pink Pussy**" was found on this unidentified F-105D. *KAHS*

Evil 'A' Skycycle III is an F-105B belonging to the 465th TFS, 507th TFG based at Tinker AFB, Oklahoma City. *Curry*

The **Dynamic Duo**, Bullwinkle and Rocky, were found on this F-105D, serial 59-0771, assigned to the 149th TFS, 192nd TFG. The photo was taken in Richmond, Virginia, September 1979. *KAHS*

White Lightning, an F-105G, serial 63-8266, was assigned to the 17th Wild Weasel Squadron in 1973, based at Korat, Thailand. The "THUD", as it is affectionately called, logged an impressive history of missions during the course of the Vietnam War. *Metz*

East Anglia Express was the name given to this F-105F belonging to the 465th TFS, 507th TFG. *Curry*

This Vietnam era nose art was on an F-105D, Thunderchief, named **Pussy Galore,** a name used in the James Bond movie, Goldfinger. The art was painted by the pilot of the aircraft Capt. "Vic" Viscarra. *Mikesh*

This F-105D, of the Kansas ANG, serial 62-4387, was named **Devil's Angel.** The art illustrates the conception that the Grim Reaper certainly was acquainted with, or related to, the Devil's Angel. *Russell*

The authors are interested in any military or civilian aviation photographs you may have on aircraft from around the world, and during all time periods. If you would like to send us your photos great care will be taken in making copies and sending them back to you. You will of course be credited should your photos be used in a future project.

John M. Campbell
Photography Archives
5405 Bodine Dr. Suite A-6
Oklahoma City, OK 73135
Dedicated to Preserving Our Photographic Heritage
of Aviation History